Footprints in Time

Dr Andrew C S Koh

Published by Dr Andrew C S Koh Publishing, 2024.

Copyright

Footprints in Time: A Journey of Nostalgia
Copyright © 2024 by Dr Andrew C S Koh
All rights reserved. No part of this book may be reproduced, stored in a retrieval system, or transmitted in any form or by any means, electronic, mechanical, photocopying, recording, or otherwise, without the prior written permission of the author, except for brief quotations embodied in critical articles or reviews.
For information or permissions, please contact:
Dr Andrew C S Koh
andrewcskoh@duck.com
Cover design and illustrations by Dr Andrew C S Koh
This book is a work of memoir and personal reflection. Any resemblance to actual persons, living or dead is purely coincidental unless otherwise stated.

Scan the QR Code above to get a free e-book

Scan the QR code above to get a review copy of Footprints in Time

Table of Contents

To my beloved wife, Wai Yin, whose love and unwavering
support have been the foundation of everything I do.

To my sons, who have brought joy and purpose into my life.

To my daughters-in-law, who have enriched our family with
their warmth and kindness.

To my grandsons and granddaughters, the light of my life,
who remind me daily of the beauty and wonder of the world.

And above all, to the glory of God, whose grace has guided me
through every step of my journey.

This book is for you all.

"Each footprint holds a story, of the roads we've walked, the loves we've cherished, and the grace that carried us through."

Foreword

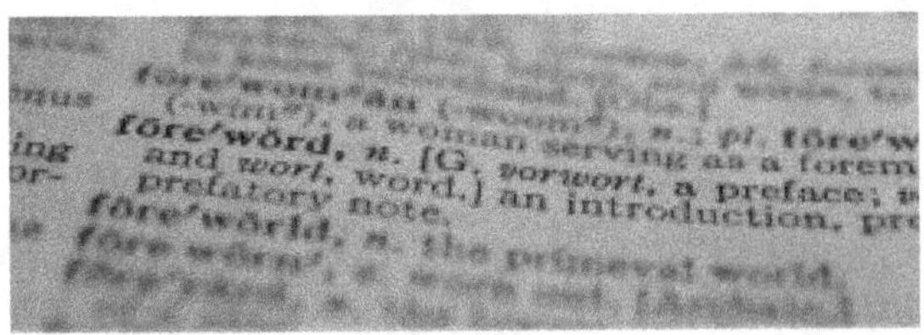

In the quiet corners of our minds, there are short moments that, although quick, make a lasting impact on our lives. These cherished memories mold our identities and forge deep connections to significant experiences, individuals, and places.

"Footprints in Time: A Journey of Nostalgia" beautifully captures the essence of cherished memories. As we navigate through life, time races forward, often leaving us in its wake. However, if we take a moment to reflect, we can follow the footprints of our own unique journey.

This book encourages us to pause, reflect, and reconnect with the past that shapes our identity today. Nostalgia is a profound experience, as it not only preserves our memories but also imparts valuable insights about the present. The author's life story combines memories of youth, important lessons, and cherished moments, creating a touching reflection.

Reflection uncovers the profound significance of our lives and the bonds we forge with both people and places. In the subsequent pages, you will encounter not just a personal narrative but a shared experience that resonates universally. It's a journey for anyone who has looked back at their past and discovered beauty in its imperfections.

These narratives extend beyond the author's influence. They belong to each of us. We all leave our unique marks on time, reflecting the years and key moments that shape our lives. The author shares nostalgic memories that connect with your own experiences. Each story is a gateway to lessons learned, joy experienced, and lasting connections that illuminate our paths through life's journey. Embrace these reflections and discover the profound impact of memories in your own life.

Pastor Peter Ku Kit Wan

23/12/2024

Preface

As we move forward, I invite you to join me as I share my memories, a journey that starts long before I wore a white coat and stethoscope. "Footprints in Time: A Journey of Nostalgia" is more than just another entry in my writing journey; it serves as a profoundly personal companion to my earlier works, "Memoirs of a Doctor" and "From Stethoscope to Wisdom."

These 20 short stories offer vivid glimpses into my past, thoughtfully curated to encapsulate the essence of my cherished memories. They reflect my upbringing and the experiences that shaped my values, passions, and outlook on life. These stories from my childhood and adulthood are close to my heart, and I often reflect on them during quiet moments.

Every story, though concise, embodies the intricate tapestry of experiences that shape who I am. As I recount these moments, I invite you to see reflections of your own journey. While our lives are distinct, they are woven together by universal themes of joy, sorrow, laughter, and growth. It's these shared human experiences that unite us, regardless of our backgrounds or the times in which we live.

This book invites you to pause and reflect, bridging the gap between the present and the past while encouraging you to revisit your own memories. Much like footprints in the sand, these stories are ephemeral yet profoundly meaningful. They occupy a cherished space in my heart, and it is a privilege to share them with you.

Take a moment to reflect on your journey, the memories you've created, and the impact you've left behind. It is through this retrospective lens that we often discover the clarity needed to forge ahead.

I hope these stories resonate with you and evoke joyful memories of our shared experiences.

Dr Andrew C S Koh

23/12/2024

Reviews

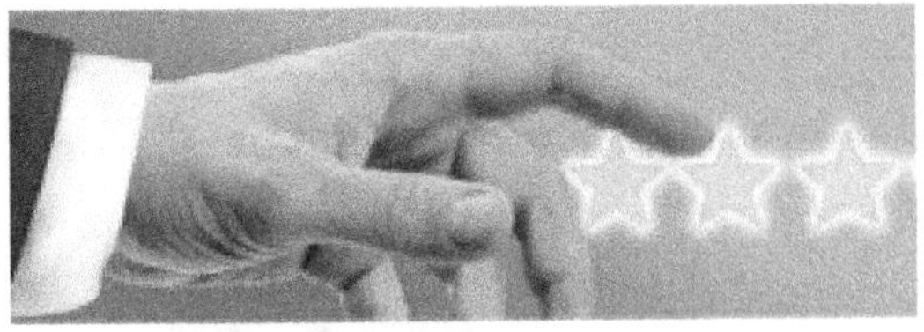

"Dr. Koh shares his humanity with readers. So detailed you feel right there with him. His beautiful family is highlighted by his wonderful words. His memoir shows that while he is an example of Godly living, he is also human." T. Townsend, Amazon

❖❖❖❖❖

"It was lovely being able to learn so much about the culture and the family life of Dr. Koh. Absolutely brilliant. Beautifully written musings." J. Surdam, Amazon

❖❖❖❖❖

"As readers dive into this book, they are sure to find themselves immersed in their own childhood memories. Shares personal experiences, including his first time sitting in the cockpit of an airplane." Emily Da Chow, Goodreads

❖❖❖❖❖

"Every chapter is cut as one slice of life, full of warmth and reminiscence. Feel the laughter, struggle, and taste the triumph. You would love this book." Nathaniel Read, Goodreads

❖❖❖❖❖

"Shares his cherished memories from many years ago. The events were enjoyable to him and brought connectivity to family and friends, and even strangers who returned to thank him." Linda Foster, Amazon

❖❖❖❖❖

"Through beautifully written prose, the author shares personal stories that are both relatable and inspiring. A must-read memoir." Karen Gurtiza, Goodreads

◇◇◇◇◇

"Each page is filled with joy, angst, and just plain living through with resilience and persistence as a good man." Rowan E. Creech, Goodreads

◇◇◇◇◇

"Shares his early life and how the Lord helped him to survive and manifest the joy that can be found in times of grief and loss." Pamela Anne, Goodreads

◇◇◇◇◇

"These stories bring inspiration and enjoyment to capture your imagination." J. Sharmani, Barnes & Noble

◇◇◇◇

"A powerful reminder to cherish our own journeys and the footprints we leave behind." Ayomide Akinfolarin, Goodreads

◇◇◇◇

"Beautifully captures pivotal moments through vivid descriptions and reflections. These memories have shaped his life. A nostalgic trip down memory lane." Yvonne Oloo, Goodreads

Chapter 1

Nostalgic Memories: My Childhood in Tanjong Malim

Prelude

The author reminisces about growing up in Tanjong Malim, Malaysia. It is a quaint town characterized by its slow pace. The community is also close-knit. Vibrant memories include enjoying coffee at local kopitiams, the joy of festivals, and heartwarming connections. These experiences taught the author the value of simplicity, relationships, and community spirit.

Nostalgic Memories

As I sit here thinking about my childhood, my thoughts return to Tanjong Malim. It's the delightful little town nestled in Malaysia. There, life seemed to flow at its own gentle pace. Growing up there felt like being in a time capsule, sheltered from the chaos of bigger cities. Tanjong Malim's sights and sounds brought back memories of carefree days spent exploring its peaceful streets. It's a place where every corner held a memory, making my heart long for those serene moments once more.

Mornings had a unique charm. They started with the rich and inviting aroma of freshly brewed coffee wafting through the air at the local kopitiam. This aroma drew neighbors together to share in lively conversations. They exchanged tales from their lives. I recall bicycles and motorbikes moving smoothly through quiet streets. These streets were lined with well-preserved pre-war shop houses. It was a nostalgic reminder of simpler times.

Each sip of coffee enhanced its rich flavor. It enriched the warm atmosphere of the surrounding community. The area was filled with laughter and friendly chatter. The clinking of mugs and the shared stories added to this sense of togetherness, making every moment feel cherished. Conversations ebbed and flowed, intertwining lives and experiences in a beautiful tapestry of connection. In that cozy space, the simple act of enjoying coffee transformed into a celebration of camaraderie and shared joy.

Weekends often featured enjoyable trips to Yik Mun Restaurant, known for its delicious dumplings that attract many visitors. If you haven't tried the local cuisine in Tanjong Malim, you're missing a vital part of its heritage! The peaceful Kuil Sri Kalikambal Hindu Temple was a perfect place for reflection for people of the Hindu faith. The calm Ulu Bernam River encouraged a deeper appreciation of nature. The combination of delicious food and stunning scenery made each visit an unforgettable experience.

The community felt enchanting, filled with a sense of warmth and familiarity, as if everyone truly knew each other. Festivals turned the neighborhood into a lively celebration, with open houses welcoming everyone. Laughter filled the lively streets as friends and families came together, enjoying each other's company.

Heartfelt conversations deepened their connections as they reminisced about the past and shared hopes for the future. In these moments, they collectively wove a tapestry of lasting memories that would be cherished for years to come. The vibrant energy of the scene was a celebration of life and unity, reflecting the warmth of their relationships.

Warm smiles and genuine interactions created a strong sense of connection and joy in the atmosphere. It was a moment where the everyday hustle faded into the background, allowing the spirit of togetherness to shine brightly. In these fleeting yet beautiful interactions, the essence of community was truly celebrated.

My time in Tanjong Malim taught me to appreciate life's simplicity and the warmth of meaningful connections. It was a special place. Even small gestures mattered greatly. Gestures like a kind smile from a stranger or a helping hand in difficult times were significant. The community's strong ties emphasized the importance of building relationships and supporting each other in our busy lives.

In a world full of distractions, these connections highlight the importance of supporting one another. By prioritizing these relationships, we can create a nurturing environment that enables us to thrive collectively. Ultimately, it becomes clear that investing in our community is just as essential as managing our individual responsibilities.

I have moved far from the small town where I grew up. The memories and experiences from that time will always stay with me. I often find myself reflecting on the simpler days, the friendships forged, and the lessons learned in that small community. Cheers to the small towns. They shape our identities and influence our life paths. They make a significant impact in subtle ways.

One happy memory is how our community came together each Chinese New Year to celebrate the annual event. The laughter, the smell of fire crackers, and the colorful lights in the night sky created a magical atmosphere. I recall celebrating Chinese New Year with family, cousins, and friends. Our excitement was palpable as we shared stories and created unforgettable moments. Those warm nights, filled with joy and camaraderie, stay etched in my heart forever.

Chapter 2

Ketoyong Road: Sweet Memories of 'Ice-Kacang'

Prelude

Ketoyong Road evokes cherished childhood memories tied to community and belonging. A standout recollection involves enjoying ice-kacang (shaved ice desert) from a legendary stall, fostering connections with friends and neighbors. These experiences show the essence of joy, nostalgia, and personal growth, emphasizing how memories shape identity and inspire future endeavors.

Ketoyong Road

Ah, Ketoyong Road! Just uttering its name evokes a delightful flood of cherished memories that I hold dear. That stretch of road in Tanjong Malim was more than just a road. It embodied the lively essence of daily life, joy, and a strong sense of community. Each moment spent there is etched in my heart, making it a truly special place in my recollections.

One particular memory shines so brightly in my mind that it feels as though it happened just yesterday. I had a classmate. His father operated an 'ice-kacang' (shaved ice) stall. The stall quickly gained a reputation for being legendary among my community. On hot afternoons, students gathered at the stall. Families and curious passersby joined them, attracted by its vibrant colors. The stall also emitted delicious smells.

The best part of my day was enjoying delicious shaved ice topped with colorful syrups. The creamy evaporated milk topping added a rich texture. Sweet corn and red beans provided a delightful twist. I always topped it up with a scoop of ice cream to make the dessert even more indulgent. The treat brought a smile to my face. It warmed my heart. Those moments became truly unforgettable.

I would sit on wooden stools, happily enjoying the refreshing icy treat as it melted in the warm air. Enjoying this delightful treat made the busy world around me feel slower. It let us savor every moment. It was so much more than just enjoying a delicious dessert. It captured the joy of spending time with friends, sharing laughter, and appreciating life's simple pleasures.

Ketoyong Road plays a vital role in my community. It links me to the town's lively people. It showcases the unique charm and rich history. I cycled down that familiar road. The refreshing wind tousled my hair. The rustling leaves above created a sense of freedom. Each pedal stroke celebrated the surroundings, evoking memories and the beauty of everyday life. At that moment, I truly felt at one with the spirit of the town.

I think back and realize the experience was memorable not just because of the delicious ice-kacang. The picturesque setting also added to it. Rather, it was the profound sense of belonging and the warmth radiating from familiar faces that truly enriched the moment.

Laughter and shared stories with family, friends and neighbors wove a strong connection in our community. The unspoken connections I made during those gatherings made each meeting feel like a special reunion. Ultimately, it was this deep-rooted feeling of connection and togetherness that transformed the ordinary into something incredibly special.

If you've ever strolled down the vibrant stretch of Ketoyong Road, you'll understand the deep connection I feel. Take a moment to savor that delightful ice-kacang and this connection becomes clear. Although life has taken me on to different paths, the cherished memories of those experiences stay in my heart. These cherished memories give me comfort. They remind me of my origin and the bonds that connect me. This remains true no matter how much time passes.

They encapsulate the essence of who I am and the experiences that have shaped my identity. No matter where life leads me, these memories will forever keep me connected to my heritage. The memories I hold reassure me that my past will always impact my future in meaningful ways.

Connecting to my history gives me a sense of continuity. It provides me with purpose. It reminds me that the lessons I've learned will guide my future decisions. The relationships I've built will also guide my future decisions. I find solace in knowing that the echoes of my past can serve as a foundation. They will support my growth and understanding in the years to come.

My experiences and future possibilities deeply enrich my life by offering valuable insights and lessons. This relationship inspires me to embrace new challenges and seize opportunities that come my way. By reflecting on where I've been, I gain the confidence to navigate uncharted territories ahead. Ultimately, this interplay between history and aspiration shapes my journey and encourages personal growth.

This was my favorite Ketoyong Road memory.

What an unforgettable moments to remember!

Chapter 3
First Day at School: A Story of Friendship

Prelude

On my first day at school, I unexpectedly found an onion in my backpack. There was also a sugar cane. This discovery sparked laughter with a new friend. His playful remark transformed my embarrassment into joy. This moment marked the beginning of a deep friendship. It provided comfort and strength. We shared experiences and faced challenges together over the years.

First Day at School

My first day at school began with an unexpected twist that I could never have anticipated. When I opened my backpack, I checked for my books and pencils. To my surprise, I found an onion and a stick of sugar cane mixed in with my usual supplies. I was puzzled by this unusual addition and wondered about its meaning. Instead of overthinking, I chose to accept the mystery, as parents often have their own reasons for their choices.

Parents often deal with complicated emotions and motivations that can be hard for children to understand. Their decisions and actions are often influenced by factors like their own upbringing, societal expectations, and personal experiences. As a child, I only saw the surface of these choices. I did not realize the deeper implications or the love and care behind them. It's a nuanced world that requires time and patience to fully understand.

I settled into my seat, getting comfortable for the journey ahead. The boy sitting next to me had bright, sparkling eyes and an infectious smile that instantly brightened the surrounding atmosphere. When he saw my strange collection of items, his eyes widened in surprise, and he couldn't help but laugh.

"Why on earth do you have an onion and sugar cane in your bag?" he asked, his amusement obvious as he tried to suppress his giggle.

I hesitated, unsure of how to express my thoughts and feelings about the situation. I was just about to say something. He gave me a big smile.

He confidently declared, "Well, onions make you smart, and sugar cane makes you sweet."

His cheerful attitude surprised me. I started to wonder if those funny ingredients could really help us deal with life's challenges!

His light hearted and playful comment transformed my embarrassment into a moment filled with laughter and joy. We spent the day talking, enjoying snacks, and laughing about my unusual school supplies. As the sun dipped below the horizon, it cast a warm golden glow. I felt like I was carrying more than just the onions and sugar cane. There was a heavier weight in my hands.

I felt a deep warmth and joy. It was a wonderful first day full of connections and friendship with a new friend. Each smile and shared laugh seemed to echo in the fading light, making this experience all the more unforgettable. The simple act of gathering these humble ingredients transformed into a cherished memory I would hold close.

It was the start of a beautiful and lasting friendship that grew stronger through shared experiences and cherished memories. This first encounter laid the foundation for a bond that would flourish, enriched by laughter, support, and countless adventures together. As the days turned into months and then years, the connection grew stronger, revealing the true beauty of companionship.

This friendship became a deep source of joy and strength, brightening the toughest times in life. It provided a comforting presence that made struggles more bearable and laughter more resonant. Together, we shared countless memories and experiences that enriched our lives and deepened our bond.

The bond we created became a source of hope. It guided us and offered comfort during the tough times we experienced together. It guided us with warmth and understanding, reminding us we were never alone, even in dark times. The support we offered each other not only helped to ease our burdens but also strengthened the bond we share. Through every challenge, this connection has truly been a source of comfort and encouragement.

Chapter 4
Spider Fights: A Childhood Reflection

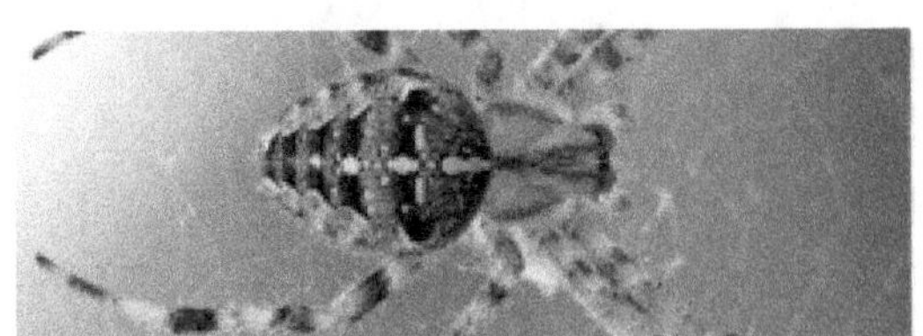

Prelude

The author reminisces about childhood spider fights, highlighting the excitement of capturing male spiders and preparing them for competition. These events fostered friendships and joy, symbolizing a blend of exploration and discovery. Ultimately, the memories show the simplicity and magic of youth, emphasizing the importance of cherishing small adventures.

Spider Fights

As a child, spider fights were one of my favorite activities, making my afternoons thrilling and fun. With a sense of adventure, I explored the bushes, carefully searching through the greenery for the best spiders. Male spiders were highly valued. They can be identified by their white faces. Female spiders with black faces were of little interest to me.

A large male spider would greatly improve its chances of success in spider fights. This advantage instill a sense of dominance and confidence for its owner. As a result, securing a larger spider is a crucial strategy for success. This highlights the crucial role of size and strength of spiders in spider fight competition.

When I caught a male spider, I would gently place it inside a matchbox. I included a few leaves to keep it comfortable. The matchbox was more than a simple container. It was a lively space where my beloved spider could explore and play. It served as a temporary home, providing a cozy space for my spider to retreat, weave webs, and feel safe.

Each time I opened it, I was reminded of the fragile balance between nature and captivity. It was a small world in a box. This matchbox held both the excitement of discovery and the comfort of familiarity for my spider and me.

As the moment for the spider fights approached, I would head to the designated meeting spot. A group of children gathered there, each proudly presenting their beloved champions. We revealed our spiders one by one. We placed two of them atop a matchbox. The spiders were poised to face off against each other.

The battle commenced as they collided with their claws, engaging in a fierce struggle for supremacy. Everyone would watch in rapt attention, cheering for their spider. The match would end when one spider disengaged and ran away, leaving the other as the victor.

The competitive battles we faced were fierce but always filled with laughter and the warmth of shared childhood memories. Reflecting on those days, I see they were about more than just exciting spider fights. They captured the joy of exploration and discovery. Those moments were not about winning or losing. They were more about the friendships formed from simple joys. I was excited to watch my little spider compete in a fight.

During these seemingly ordinary moments, I truly began to appreciate the magic of my childhood. The simplicity of those moments allowed me to revel in the wonder and joy I often took for granted.

Every adventure, no matter how small, created cherished memories of the innocence and imagination of my youth. In retrospect, those fleeting instances of happiness reveal the true magic of youth.

Chapter 5
Spinning Top: A Symbol of Joy and Connection

Prelude

The spinning top game from my childhood evokes joy and cherished memories of carefree play with friends. Each vibrant top symbolized beauty and excitement, captivating me as it spun. These experiences shaped my growth, highlighting the importance of connections and simple pleasures. They stay treasured reminders of innocence and life's fleeting beauty.

Spinning Top

Spinning top was one of my favorite games as a child, adding excitement and happiness to my playtime. These tops were far from ordinary toys. They were crafted with meticulous care, often adorned with vibrant, eye-catching paint that made each one unique and beautiful.

I tightly wound the top with thread. Then, I quickly flicked my wrist to release it onto the ground. The top spun gracefully on its pointed nail, captivating me with its balance and motion. As it spun, the colors and patterns on its surface blurred together, enhancing its enchanting movement. I watched in awe, amazed by the simple yet captivating dance of physics.

Each spin immersed me in a captivating world where time paused, letting me fully enjoy the magic of the moment. With each rotation, I felt reality fade away, drawing me into a world of vibrant colors and captivating sensations. I felt a sense of pure bliss and wonder as the ordinary boundaries of life disappeared. In that brief escape, nothing else mattered but the exhilarating joy of the experience.

Soon, other players would join in, each spinning their own tops with impressive skill and a palpable sense of excitement. The scene came alive with a burst of color and motion as the tops spun together on the ground. The joyful sound of spinning and friends' laughter created an atmosphere of happiness and friendship. It was an absolutely breathtaking sight that left an indelible mark on my memory, one that I will cherish forever.

The moment's beauty was so profound that it still brings me joy today. Thinking about this experience always makes me smile, reminding me of the amazing feelings I had. Those cherished moments are a priceless treasure that remind me of the joy and connection they brought to my life. They highlight the profound impact these experiences had on my growth and development as an individual.

Reflecting on them brings me immense gratitude and appreciation for the people and circumstances that shaped those experiences. Their presence and influence are crucial to my journey, shaping my experiences and growth. Their contributions add depth and complexity to the narrative of my life, enriching it in ways I often consider.

Each interaction and shared moment helps to weave a more intricate tapestry of memories, highlighting the importance of these connections. The experiences and people in my life add depth and meaning to my journey, enriching my story. Each moment, whether joyful or challenging, adds layers of understanding and growth that shape who I am.

The connections I've made and the lessons I've learned are invaluable, creating a narrative that is both unique and significant. My life is more than just a series of events. It has become a meaningful story full of experiences. These experiences and lessons are worth sharing.

Each chapter shares insights and emotions that highlight my journey, showcasing the connections and transformations I've experienced. It's a story that reflects who I am and encourages deeper engagement from others. This tale is not only mine but also a testament to the universal experiences that bind people together.

Spinning top was more than just a game. They represented joy, skill, friendship, and the simple pleasures that united the community. The laughter shared and the competitive spirit that filled the air created an unparalleled sense of community. Those vivid memories are a cherished part of my childhood, reminding me of carefree days in the sun.

Each spin of the top brings back fond memories of simpler, joyful times. I cherish these memories because they remind me of my childhood's joy and innocence. These memories shaped who I am today. The spinning top signifies the precious moments I cherish, reminding me to appreciate the passage of time. It serves as a delightful reminder of life's transient beauty and the importance of those cherished moments.

Chapter 6
Unity and Strength: The Tanjong Malim Flood

Prelude

The severe flood in Tanjong Malim during the 1960s transformed the community. It showcased nature's unpredictable power. It also highlighted its profound impact on lives. The disaster united residents, fostering resilience and camaraderie. People supported each other through shared experiences. This demonstrated how collective strength can help overcome individual struggles during adversity. It led to newfound hope and solidarity.

Tanjong Malim Flood

The memory of the severe flood in Tanjong Malim in the 1960s stays clear in my mind. It serves as a strong reminder of nature's unpredictable power. A once peaceful town was dramatically changed when heavy rains caused the river to overflow. Safe, dry streets turned into rushing streams, and many homes were flooded, creating chaos and despair.

That day profoundly affected the community, changing lives and reshaping the landscape for years to come. Families and the neighborhood were deeply influenced as people united to cope with emotional scars and physical changes. This event affected individual lives and the community's spirit, resulting in new beginnings and a stronger sense of resilience.

The memories of that important day reminded me of my shared history. They also reminded me of the strength I found in each other during tough times. It was a shared experience that showcased my struggles and strengthened the bonds formed while overcoming challenges together. I realized that solidarity was a source of strength and inspiration for each other. Ultimately, it was a celebration of unity in the face of hardship, emphasizing the importance of camaraderie in overcoming obstacles.

During those difficult times, people united. They helped one another move their belongings to safer areas. They prioritized everyone's safety amid the chaos. Neighbors supported each other, demonstrating a strong sense of unity and cooperation. Amid the chaos, the community's actions strengthened our bonds and reminded us that we weren't alone in facing challenges.

The experience showcased resilience, turning a challenging situation into an opportunity for solidarity and real friendships. In the face of adversity, we came together, showcasing our strength and determination to support one another. This transformation helped us tackle challenges and build deeper connections through shared experiences and understanding.

It highlighted how uniting in difficult times can lead to positive results. Unity in tough times fosters resilience and builds a sense of community and shared purpose. Witnessing such collaboration reinforces the idea that collective strength can overcome individual struggles. Indeed, it highlights the importance of supporting one another during these difficult moments in life.

The devastating flood significantly affected both the town's landscape and the memories of those who experienced it. It highlighted nature's power to instantly change lives and environments. It also showcased the human compassion and resilience that often arise in tough times.

Despite the challenges we faced, our community united beautifully, showing that hope and solidarity can thrive even in tough times. People from all walks of life contributed their time, resources, and support, showing an incredible commitment to one another. This collective spirit not only lifted our morale but also reinforced the idea that we are stronger together. We demonstrated that adversity can bring out our best, and together, we can overcome any challenge.

My house underwent severe damage by the flood incident, leaving everything in total disarray and ruin. Almost all the furniture inside was either destroyed or rendered unusable, adding to the distress of the situation. The task of cleaning up proved to be quite a challenge. Coping with the loss took a lot of physical effort and emotional strength.

The flood reminded me that God has ultimate control over nature and that humanity can't control its unpredictable forces. God's grace and mercy bring moments of peace and serenity, helping me find tranquility even in chaos. I must take time to sincerely thank God when life is going well. I must never take God's presence or His blessings for granted, as they are the foundation of my well-being.

Chapter 7
Tragedy: A Tale of Fear and Loss

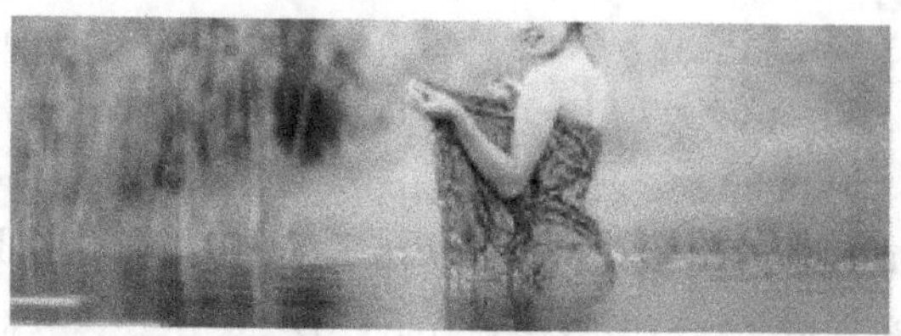

Prelude

In Tanjong Malim in the 1970s, locals shared a scary story that some older residents still remember well. A Malay woman was washing clothes by the banks of the Ulu Bernam River. During that particular era, people followed a common daily routine that often revolved around their interactions with the surrounding nature. One day, a crocodile suddenly emerged from the river and attacked the woman. In an instant, it swallowed the woman alive in front of the terrified community.

A Tale of Fear and Loss

This frightening event traumatized the residents, leaving them with lasting fear and sadness. The incident highlighted the hidden dangers in daily life that often go unnoticed. It highlighted the reality that seemingly mundane routines harbor unexpected risks that can disrupt the sense of safety. This unsettling event compelled people to think about their surroundings and question what other threats they are oblivious to.

It emphasized the importance of staying vigilant and aware in a rapidly changing and unpredictable environment. This awareness not only helps in navigating challenges but also in seizing opportunities that arise unexpectedly. By fostering a mindset of attentiveness and adaptability, we can better prepare ourselves for whatever lies ahead.

Such diligence is essential in ensuring success and resilience in the face of change.

This tragic incident reminded me of the many dangers in nature. It revealed how unpredictable and dangerous the environment can be. It underscored the importance of respecting nature and recognizing the inherent risks linked to its beauty. During a time when humanity was still learning to coexist with nature, people needed more understanding. They also needed more caution. Ultimately, this tragedy became a lesson that resonated deeply within the community.

The news shocked the community, leaving residents in fear and disbelief over the sudden change in their situation. The Ulu Bernam River, once vital for local communities, has become a source of fear and caution, impacting daily life. It transformed from a resource-rich fishing spot into a symbol of uncertainty and danger, disrupting the region's former harmony. This change has significantly affected how people engage with their surroundings, making them more alert in their daily activities.

The river was once a vital lifeline for the community. Sadly, it has become a symbol of shifting dynamics. It reflects changing relationships among its people. Its waters, once filled with laughter and life, now show the struggles and challenges faced by the residents. This transformation symbolizes loss and the effects of change, leaving a lasting impression on those who recall its former glory. The river serves as a reminder of the past, stirring feelings of nostalgia and longing.

After this unsettling event, the community elders continued to share this story with the younger generations. This was to emphasize the importance of staying vigilant near riverbanks. This story reminds people to appreciate nature's blessings while being aware of its potential dangers. Natural wonders can quickly become dangerous if people are not vigilant.

These lessons emphasize the importance of respecting nature's unpredictability and being cautious of its dangers. Understanding that natural forces can be both beautiful and terrifying helps us recognize our limitations as humans. It reminds us to approach the environment with humility and mindfulness, always prepared for the unexpected.

Increased awareness helps us form a deeper connection with nature, enhancing our appreciation for its beauty and complexity. Cultivating a bond with nature increases awareness. This awareness leads to a greater sense of safety and well-being. People better understand and navigate their environment. This relationship enhances outdoor experiences and promotes the responsibility to protect the environment for future generations. Thus, cultivating this awareness can significantly enrich both personal experiences and the broader ecological community.

The details of this tragic story still resonates with the local community. It was a sad story that has become a part of the community's history, leaving a lasting impact. The memories of this event reminded me of the sorrow and strength of those affected. It's a haunting reminder of how such memories can persist long after the events have transpired.

Chapter 8

Nostalgic Adventure: My Robinson Crusoe Tree House

Prelude

The author reflects on his childhood experience of building a tree house in Tanjong Malim, inspired by Robinson Crusoe. This cozy sanctuary served as a creative escape, filled with books and tranquility. Over the years, it became a symbol of imagination and peaceful solitude, now fading but cherished in nostalgic memories.

Robinson Crusoe Tree House

My Robinson Crusoe Tree House was located in my childhood home's large backyard in Tanjong Malim. It was my favorite place to escape and relax. The entire process of planning, sawing, and hammering took me several weeks of dedicated effort and youthful enthusiasm. It stood ten feet tall in the tree branches. I built it from salvaged wooden planks from old crates and discarded materials. This tree house wasn't just a structure; it was a testament to my creativity and resourcefulness during those formative years.

My Tree House was inspired by Robinson Crusoe, the resourceful sailor known for his survival skills. It was my personal sanctuary. It provided a place to escape the chaos of the outside world. It was far from distractions that fueled my imagination. Sitting in the branches, I only heard the distant noise of life below. It reminded me of the vibrant world outside my peaceful space. It was a place where I could think about, dream, and connect with my adventurous spirit.

My cozy cabin among the trees was accessible by a charming, simple ladder that enhances its rustic appeal. Though the space was limited, and I couldn't fully stretch out, that minor inconvenience was of little concern to me. The cozy room had shelves overflowing with my favorite books. These included exciting adventure novels, intriguing mysteries, and vast sci-fi epics. They transported me to other worlds. Every morning, I loved watching the sunrise through a small window. It lit up my garden. It created a calm start to the day.

Afternoons were the perfect time for me to relax and escape into a good book. I loved the calming sound of pages rustling in the breeze. It reminded me of a jungle. I imagined myself as Robinson Crusoe, embarking on a survival adventure. The reading retreat often felt like a peaceful sanctuary, allowing my dreams and daydreams to thrive. Each afternoon brought a unique blend of excitement and tranquility, making it my favorite part of the day.

Rainy days always made me feel comforted and peaceful. The soft sound of raindrops on the roof became a beautiful melody, taking my mind to distant places. I sat cozy by the window in a warm blanket. The soothing rain guided my thoughts on imaginary adventures. These adventures were far from reality. In those moments, it felt like the outside world had paused. I could fully enjoy the peacefulness of my own little universe. The noise of daily life faded away, leaving me in a comforting silence. In this secluded space, I found solace and clarity, allowing my thoughts to roam freely. It was a blissful escape, a precious pause in the chaos of reality.

I haven't climbed into the tree house in Tanjong Malim for more than a decade. It used to bring me joy and wonder. Nature is slowly reclaiming a once vibrant structure, which now serves as a faded reminder of its former glory. Every time I return to Tanjong Malim, I cherish the memories of my imaginative adventures. I deeply felt peace alone among the trees. Those nostalgic moments remind me of a simpler time, steeped in the beauty of nature and whimsical dreams.

The Robinson Crusoe Tree House I built will always be special to me. It signifies a unique time in my life. During that time, I created my own world filled with imagination and adventure. I hammered every nail and chose each branch. This meticulous work created a personal space. It became a place where I could escape the chaos of daily life. It showcased my creativity and youthful spirit, reminding me of the joy of creating something meaningful. Whenever I look back on that time, I am filled with nostalgia for the freedom and possibilities it represented.

Chapter 9
The Fabulous Four: My Beloved Pets

Prelude

The author's childhood was profoundly influenced by their pets, who were considered family. Each animal brought unique joys, like Bobby's loyalty, Kitty's elegance, Adam's curiosity, and Grace's warmth. Together, they created cherished memories filled with love and laughter. These experiences shaped the author's identity. They taught him enduring lessons about friendship and connection.

The Fabulous Four

As a child, my home was filled with happy voices, cheerful barks, and calming purrs from my cherished pets. They were not merely pets to me. They were essential members of my family, bringing companionship and love to my joyful world full of adventures and laughter. Bobby's playful spirit added joy. Kitty's graceful elegance brought beauty. Adam's calming presence introduced peace. Grace's quirky antics made me laugh. Together, they brightened even the gloomiest days.

They significantly influenced my childhood, creating a treasured collection of joyful and warm memories. Each shared moment, each laughter-filled day, crafted a tapestry of experiences that I hold dear. The bonds we formed created a safe haven where I could freely explore the world around me. Reflecting back, I realize just how invaluable those experiences are to me today.

Bobby, my loyal Alsatian mix, was the guardian of our home, offering us safety and comfort. His scruffy coat and bright, alert eyes gave him the look of a seasoned watchman, always ready for action. His distinct bark alerted me when someone approached the gate or when the postman stayed too long. Yet, beneath his tough exterior, Bobby had a heart of gold. He would faithfully follow me everywhere, his tail wagging happily to show his love and loyalty.

Then there was Kitty, my sleek and elegant cat, who effortlessly graced our home with her presence. She had the softest brown fur that seemed to shimmer in the light. Her distinct love for sunbathing on the windowsill brought a unique charm to my life. Bobby was energetic and loyal, while Kitty offered a calm and compelling presence. She would often curl up beside me during moments of reading or daydreaming. Her purring is soothing, but her aloofness hides her mischievous side. She often steals bites of my dinner when she thinks I was not watching.

My playful monkeys brought both chaos and laughter into my life, always keeping me on my toes. Adam, the older of the two, assumed the role of the self-proclaimed leader, displaying a curious and charming personality. His curiosity drove him to explore everything. He explored from bananas in the fruit basket to the shiny buttons on my shirt. He found these fascinating. I once saw him amusingly trying to "read" my schoolbooks, flipping through the pages as if he understood everything.

Grace, the younger female, was the gentler of the two. She often sought comfort by clinging to my arm like a loving child. Her big, expressive eyes seemed to capture every detail of my actions, full of curiosity and warmth. Unlike Adam, who thrived on playful moments, Grace enjoyed quiet moments. She would often sit happily beside me, eating bananas while our friends Bobby and Kitty slept peacefully nearby.

The fabulous four, each with their unique quirks and personalities, created a lively household filled with joy and laughter. I will always treasure those sunny afternoons in the backyard. I watched Bobby chase his tail and Kitty swat at butterflies. Adam and Grace swung joyfully from the tree branches above. They were not just pets. They were my beloved playmates, trusted companions, and sometimes my mischievous partners as we embarked on our adventures. Each moment spent with them contributed to an unforgettable tapestry of memories that I hold dear to my heart.

Though my beloved pets are gone, their memories are still vivid in my mind. Bobby's fierce and protective bark still echoes, while the soothing sound of Kitty's gentle purrs brings warmth to my heart. I remember Adam's fun antics that always made me laugh and Grace's quiet support that comforted me on tough days. These beloved companions influenced my life greatly. They taught me important lessons about love and loyalty. I also learned the simple joys of true friendship from them.

Reflecting on those times, I came to understand that they were much more than mere animals. They were essential to my childhood, each shaping my experiences and contributing to who I am today. They were not just friends but also sources of joy and comfort during my youth, creating cherished memories. Every moment with them feels like a special chapter in my life. It is filled with laughter, valuable lessons, and deep love. I will always treasure these moments.

These experiences are not just fleeting instances. They are the remarkable threads that weave together the tapestry of my existence, reminding me of the beauty of connection. Each shared adventure and heartfelt conversation adds depth to my journey, making it truly unforgettable.

I am grateful for every moment I've experienced, as they have created cherished memories that I will always treasure. These experiences, both big and small, shape who I am and add richness to my journey. The significance of these memories resonates deeply within me, reminding me of the beauty life has to offer. Every moment will always hold a special place in my heart, reminding me of the time well spent.

Chapter 10
Camping Under the Stars: The Boy Scout Experience

Prelude

The author reflects on their meaningful experiences in the Boy Scouts, highlighting valuable lessons in teamwork, leadership, and responsibility. Camping trips at Sungei Bill fostered connections with friends, creating lasting memories filled with joy, camaraderie, and appreciation for nature. These moments enhanced their character and instilled a profound sense of community and belonging.

Scouting and Camping

In school, I joined the Boy Scouts, where I developed skills and learned important values like teamwork, leadership, and perseverance. Being part of this organization allowed me to enjoy outdoor activities. I participated in community service projects. I also embarked on exciting adventures that enhanced my childhood. The experiences I gained from scouting were not just enjoyable. They played a significant role in shaping my character and instilling a sense of responsibility.

My time in the Boy Scouts was a meaningful part of my school life that I still cherish. The experiences, friendships, and valuable life lessons I gained during that time have significantly shaped who I am today. Every camping trip, badge earned, and shared adventure is special to me, highlighting the value of teamwork and community.

Thinking about those moments fills me with nostalgia and gratitude for the amazing journey I shared with my fellow scouts.

During the school holidays, it was the Scout movement's tradition to go camping at the beautiful Sungei Bill Campsite. We aim to arrive early to maximize our time. So, after a smooth trip, we quickly set up our tents in the beautiful surroundings. The excitement of being in nature and the anticipation of our outdoor adventures make the experience even more special.

Participating in such activities together helps me to relax and bond, creating lasting memories that enhance our experience. Time away from daily life helped me and my fellow scouts to connect more deeply. This collective relaxation helps me to recharge while also nurturing the friendships that were so important to my scouting journey.

These moments greatly improve my sense of community and teamwork, strengthening my connection with others. They create opportunities for collaboration and shared experiences that strengthen our bonds. Through these shared challenges and triumphs, I feel more integrated into the group. This sense of unity not only enriched my personal experiences but also elevated the collective spirit of teamwork.

In the evening, we enjoyed cooking our own dinner. We prepared our meal and took it to a scenic spot by the campsite. We enjoyed it while sitting on the large, smooth rocks by the riverside. While enjoying our meal, the soothing sounds of flowing water and rustling leaves enhanced our dining experience.

Dinner at the campsite was an unforgettable experience. I enjoyed delicious food with the beauty of nature in a peaceful outdoor setting. The soft sounds of nature complemented the delicious meal, creating a perfect harmony that made the night even more special. Surrounded by lush greenery and under the open sky, every moment felt magical and serene. It was an extraordinary way to embrace both culinary delights and the soothing embrace of the great outdoors.

After a pleasant dinner, we gathered around the campfire, enjoying the warmth and cozy atmosphere. As the fire crackled and danced, we sang our favorite campfire songs. *"Kumbayah"* and *"It Only Takes a Spark"* accompanied by the strumming of guitars, resonated through the air. These songs brought smiles and a sense of community. We also engaged in lively games and heartfelt sharing, exchanging testimonies that deepened our connections.

The experience brought me great joy and warmth, creating lasting memories under a beautiful starlit sky. The twinkling stars above created a magical atmosphere, making our time together even more special. The night was filled with stories and laughter, creating unforgettable moments that I will always remember.

It was a delightful evening. Laughter and warmth filled the air. The gathering brought everyone closer together. It created stronger connections among the attendees. The night's shared moments and warm conversations created lasting memories for everyone. The atmosphere was charged with joy and camaraderie, making it a truly unforgettable experience.

After enjoying the campfire, we took turns watching over our campsite throughout the quiet night until dawn. We carefully tended to the fire's embers to keep it alive, providing warmth and comfort against the cold. To fight fatigue and lift our spirits, we drank strong black coffee, which helped us stay alert. We shared stories and laughter under the stars, enjoying our time in the woods.

I heard a unique symphony at night in the jungle, made up of buzzing insects, singing birds, and hooting owls. It felt as if the jungle itself was alive, weaving together a tapestry of nature's melodies that captivated my senses. I looked at the night sky and felt amazed by the beauty of God's creation. The glowing moon especially illuminated the landscape.

The stars twinkled like diamonds on a dark canvas, lighting up the beautiful wilderness around me. Each constellation told its own story, inviting me to ponder the wonders of the universe. As I stood there, the beauty of nature surrounded me, and the twinkling cosmos above created an unforgettable, soul-touching experience.

The soft rustle of leaves and the gentle chirping of birds created a peaceful atmosphere throughout the landscape. I looked up at the night sky and saw each star shining brightly. Each star told its own unique story. They all added to the magic of the moment. The combination of nature's sounds and the celestial show above filled me with a sense of wonder and peace.

This experience made me feel a deep connection to the universe, enhancing my sense of unity with it. It created a moment where time felt like it paused, letting me fully experience the now. At that moment, my worries faded, and I felt a sense of peace and belonging. It was truly a remarkable reminder of the vastness of life and my place within it.

Chapter 11
Mid-Autumn Festival: The Joy of Moon Cakes and Lanterns

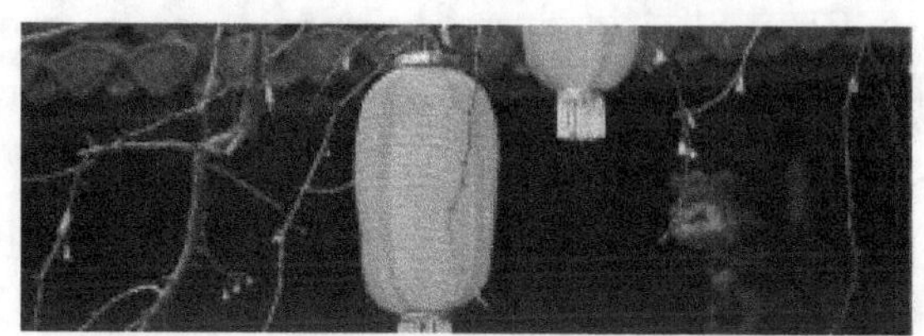

Prelude

The Mid-Autumn Festival is celebrated on the 15th Day of the Chinese Lunar month. It unites families and friends under the full moon. They create cherished memories through lanterns and moon cakes. Festivities include storytelling, artistic displays, and delicious feasts. These activities highlight the joy of togetherness. They also emphasize the significance of shared experiences and cultural traditions.

Moon Cakes and Lanterns

The Mid-Autumn Festival is also known as the Moon Cake or Lantern Festival. It is celebrated on the 15th Day of the Chinese Lunar month. It is a wonderful festival. It brought my family and friends together. We created lasting memories under the bright full moon. Those magical evenings brought joy and warmth. I cherish them as some of my happiest childhood moments. They were filled with laughter, bright colors, and the sweet smell of freshly baked moon cakes.

Each celebration uniquely merged rich traditions and captivating storytelling. This blend created an unforgettable atmosphere of shared joy and happiness throughout the festival. These elements connect to honor the past and create a sense of community among participants. Every moment of celebration created a meaningful experience, leaving lasting memories for everyone to cherish. It was this exceptional combination that truly made the festival an extraordinary event in the lives of all who attended.

The sun set, casting a warm glow. My siblings, cousins, and friends gathered in the front yard. Each of us held our unique lanterns. With every passing year, our creativity flourished, resulting in increasingly imaginative designs beyond our wildest dreams. The lanterns had playful shapes like dragons, rabbits, and goldfish.

They also featured elegant designs inspired by stars, flowers, and geometric patterns. These elements highlighted our artistic creativity. The soft glow of candlelight lit up our paper creations. Enchanting shadows danced on the ground. It added a magical feel as we happily walked through our neighborhood.

As we walked through the lively streets, colorful lights and cheerful voices created a delightful atmosphere. The older kids confidently led with their larger, intricately designed lanterns. The younger ones followed, holding their simpler but charming creations. We joyfully sang traditional songs and shared our artistic efforts with everyone we met. Families gathered outside. Our faces were bright with warmth and happiness. The festive parade made the whole town seem to come alive.

After the lively parade, we returned home to enjoy a wonderful feast. My mother and aunts created a stunning table. It was filled with delicious treats like moon cakes, candied lotus seeds, ripe pomelos, and fragrant sticky rice cakes. I remember the excitement I felt when I sliced into the moon cakes. I saw their rich fillings of lotus paste and sweet red bean. There was also the tasty surprise of salted egg yolk inside. The combination of flavors and aromas made the celebration even more memorable, turning the feast into a cherished experience.

The younger kids excitedly raced to see who could peel their pomelos the fastest, laughing as they competed. Meanwhile, the adults gathered nearby, fondly recalling their own Mid-Autumn celebrations from the past. The warm scent of freshly brewed tea filled the air. It created a cozy atmosphere as my grandparents served each cup. They encouraged everyone to take a moment to relax and enjoy the experience. The fun competition and warm nostalgia created a joyful and united atmosphere, making the celebration even more special.

That evening, we gathered in the peaceful garden under the bright full moon, which illuminated us with its silver light. My grandfather often entertained us with charming stories. One was the legend of Change, the moon goddess. Her faithful companion, the jade rabbit, is said to live on the moon.

As we enjoyed the moonlight, we learned in to share our hopes and dreams. We whispered our wishes to the night, hoping it would send them into the universe. In that special moment with loved ones and nature around us, we felt a strong sense of unity. We hoped for our dreams to become reality.

The Mid-Autumn Festival wasn't merely a celebration filled with vibrant lanterns or exquisite moon cakes. It was a heartfelt occasion that symbolized togetherness and unity among family and friends. It allowed us to create lasting memories that I deeply cherish. The warm glow of a lantern and the sweet taste of moon cake remind me of joyful nights. These nights are filled with love and laughter from the special people in my life.

These moments are etched in my memory, a beautiful tapestry woven from shared stories and cherished experiences. The atmosphere during those evenings was always electric, filled with a sense of togetherness that I hold dear. Simple reminders can stir deep emotions and a longing for joyful moments with loved ones.

These cherished memories enhance my appreciation for this beautiful festival. They help me think about the joy and connection it brings to friends and family. They serve as poignant reminders of the warmth and togetherness that such celebrations bring to our lives.

Shared laughter and love strengthen our bonds and create lasting happiness.

Embracing these memories, I feel a greater appreciation for the strong community and joy this festival signifies. The connections formed, and the joy shared among friends and family during this time truly highlight the importance of togetherness. This festival not only brings back nostalgic feelings but also reinforces the bonds that unite us all. I am increasingly grateful for the experiences and relationships that make this celebration special.

Chapter 12

Chinese New Year: Fire Crackers and Ang Pow Packets

Prelude

Chinese New Year is a cherished celebration filled with traditions that evoke joy and family unity. The fifteen-day festival includes festive gatherings, vibrant decorations, and delightful meals, fostering a sense of renewal. Children's excitement is highlighted by receiving Ang Pows and celebrating with firecrackers, creating lasting memories and deepening cultural bonds.

Fire Crackers and Ang Pow Packets

Chinese New Year was always a joyful and exciting time filled with traditions over the fifteen days of celebration. As a child, it was my favorite time of year. It was filled with family gatherings, colorful decorations, and delicious meals. These elements created a warm and festive atmosphere. Everything felt brighter and rejuvenated, as if the world was offering new opportunities. Each day brought its own unique customs, further deepening my appreciation for this culturally rich and heartwarming holiday.

The excitement built weeks before the festival as my parents took me on shopping trips, hinting at new beginnings. We visited many stores. We searched for new clothes, shoes, and socks. We wanted to capture the spirit of renewal for the New Year. On New Year's Day, I woke up early. I wore my bright red outfit. It made me feel renewed. I was ready to embrace the year with enthusiasm and hope. The experience was about more than just the outfits; it represented a fresh start and creating lasting family memories.

We celebrated with cheerful exclamations of "Gong Xi Fa Cai!" while sharing heartfelt wishes and blessings with family and friends, making the atmosphere warm and joyful. For us children, the true excitement came from a delightful surprise. It was the small red packets, known as Ang Pows. We happily received Ang Pows from parents, uncles, aunts, and distant relatives, each sharing them with smiles and kind words. As we opened the ang pows, we found cash in brand-new currency notes. To a child, it felt like a fortune. This discovery sparked our imaginations and dreams.

I clutched our growing stash of Ang Pows with excitement and anticipation. I treated them as if they were precious golden tickets. They held the key to my fantastical plans. My cousins and I quickly decided to spend our windfall on firecrackers. We cheerfully pooled our money. Then, we went to the nearest shop to choose sparklers and firecrackers. Our goal was to light up the night sky. We felt joy and camaraderie. We anticipated the exciting displays we would create together. Our planning felt like an unfolding adventure.

As night fell, the sky became a vibrant show of colors and captivating sounds that energized the atmosphere. We excitedly lit firecrackers, laughing and shrieking as the pops, fizzles, and loud booms echoed through the neighborhood. The adults scolded us for getting too close to the dazzling sparks. Yet, their joyful smiles showed they enjoyed the show. Their twinkling eyes revealed their delight as much as ours. It was a magical time. Youthful energy filled the air. Each explosion united us in a moment of joy and wonder.

The festivities extended delightfully beyond just a single night, immersing us in joyous celebrations for an entire fifteen days. Throughout this period, we eagerly traversed various neighborhoods.

We visited relatives both near and far. Each occasion provided a new opportunity to fill our pockets with the coveted Ang Pows.

As children, we acted as strategists, carefully planning our routes and estimating the rewards we could gather on each outing. Each stop offered a chance to gather more ang pows. We enjoyed an array of delectable snacks. These included pineapple tarts, crispy peanut cookies, and piles of sweet mandarin oranges. This made the experience even more enjoyable.

The joy of Chinese New Year still lingered in our hearts after fifteen wonderful days. The scent of firecrackers filled the air. We enjoyed festive treats together. This celebration was not merely marked by new clothes, fire crackers, and ang pows. It was far more profound. It included the laughter in our homes.

We cherished family reunions. The traditions connected us through our shared heritage and love. Every moment in this joyful atmosphere highlighted the strong bonds that connect us as a family. These bonds also strengthen our community. They make the festival unforgettable.

Firecrackers and red ang pows filled with money remind me of my happy, carefree childhood. Chinese New Year is a joyful celebration that reflects simplicity and tranquility, highlighted by vibrant decorations and clothing. This festival is rooted in traditions passed down through generations, showcasing Chinese cultural heritage. It creates a strong sense of community as families and friends unite to honor their ancestors and celebrate together. Chinese New Year brings people together, fostering strong bonds and lasting memories.

Those moments were joyful and exciting, filled with endless future possibilities. It brings back memories of a time when life felt full of possibilities, and every celebration became an exciting adventure. Each event was infused with a sense of joy and discovery, making moments cherished and unforgettable. I recall the excitement and anticipation that accompanied each gathering, as if they were gateways to new experiences and friendships. Those were precious times that seemed to stretch on forever, filled with laughter and boundless enthusiasm.

Chapter 13

Flying Kites: Unforgettable Childhood Memories

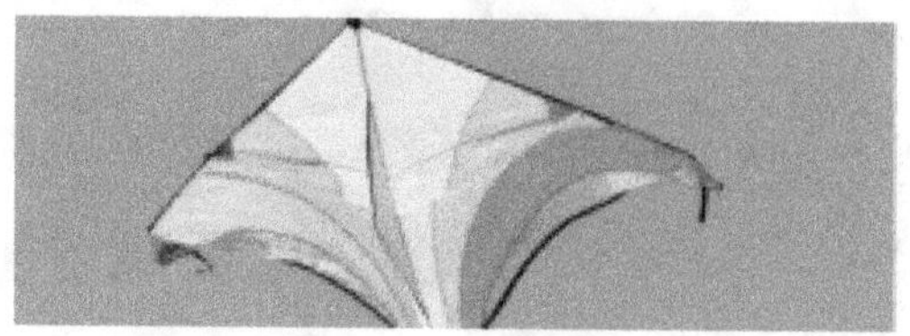

Prelude

The joy of kite making and flying is portrayed as a cherished childhood activity that symbolizes creativity and freedom. Each unique kite shows the maker's personality, while the process fosters memories and teamwork. Friendly competitions enhance community bonds, emphasizing shared experiences and the joy of connecting with others through this delightful pastime.

Kite Making and Flying

As a child, I loved making kites. It was an easy and rewarding process. You just needed two bamboo sticks for the frame. You also required some string for flying and a colorful paper for the sail. Every kite I created was a unique representation of my personality, showcasing my vibrant colors, intricate designs, and creative spirit.

Letting it go into the sky filled me with joy. Watching it gracefully dance among the clouds gave me a sense of freedom. There was something magical about seeing my creations float high above, as they mirrored my hopes and dreams. Each flight was not just a moment of fun but also a beautiful expression of who I was inside.

Building and flying kites was about the memories I made. It was about the excitement I experienced, not just the end result or the kite's design. Each step, from selecting materials to watching it soar in the sky, held a special significance. It was a joyful time of laughter, creativity, and teamwork, where even small setbacks enhanced our experience. Ultimately, the journey and the moments I shared were far more important than the completed kite itself.

First, I cut two bamboo sticks into thin strips. The longer for the vertical spine and a shorter one for the horizontal crosspiece. Using string, I tied the two sticks together to form a perfect cross. Then, I carefully connected the four ends of the cross with another string, creating the frame of the kite.

The most exciting part of the process followed. I chose a bright, lightweight sheet of paper that looks good and performs well in flight. I carefully glued the paper onto the structure, making sure it was smooth and taut to catch the wind properly. After a few final adjustments, I could barely contain my excitement as my kite was ready to fly!

I would take my colorful kite to a large open field on a windy day. There, the skies and winds were ideal for flying. I launched the kite into the air. I felt a rush of excitement and joy. It soared higher and higher. It would shrink in size as it rose, becoming a colorful speck against the endless blue sky. Seeing this tiny dot in the sky fills me with wonder. It gives me a sense of freedom. It's as if my spirit is being lifted with it.

Holding the string on the ground, I felt a simple magic. I was connected to something soaring and dancing freely above. Flying kites became a beloved childhood joy, sparking wonder, excitement, and adventure while filling my heart with happiness. The colorful kites in the blue sky made me feel a deep sense of freedom.

Soon, I will see others arriving with their colorful kites, excited to join the fun. Each participant will skillfully launch their kites into the vast blue sky, competing against one another in a friendly contest. The ultimate goal will be to see whose kite can soar the highest, dancing gracefully among the clouds. This competition will encourage healthy rivalry while highlighting the importance of joy, laughter, and teamwork.

Teammates will grow closer and strengthen their bonds while enjoying friendly competition. This event aims to create an inclusive environment for people to come together and have fun. It encourages sharing happy moments and building meaningful connections. I aim to create an exciting and friendly atmosphere, so everyone leaves with lasting memories. My intention is to highlight the importance of community and friendship, ultimately enhancing the overall experience for all participants. I believe that through these shared experiences, lasting bonds can be created, enriching lives in the process.

Chapter 14
From Patient to Pilot: An Unexpected Visitor

Prelude

A routine day at the clinic transforms when a former patient, now a confident pilot, visits to express gratitude. He recalled how the doctor's support during a severe illness shaped his journey. Their heartfelt reunion highlights the profound impact of compassion in healthcare, rekindling the doctor's commitment to inspire and heal.

An Unexpected Visitor

It was an utterly unremarkable day in my clinic, one that felt like time had come to a standstill. The empty waiting room felt unusually solitary. I sipped warm tea. I flipped through an old medical journal to pass the time. The soothing silence enveloped me like a gentle blanket, creating a tranquil atmosphere that initially felt comforting.

Over time, the comforting quiet turned dull and monotonous, leaving me restless and dissatisfied. I miss the lively atmosphere of an office, filled with conversation and teamwork. I missed the connection and teamwork that come from working with others. It's clear that I miss the buzz of a bustling workplace, where ideas flow freely and relationships flourish.

Without warning, a sudden knock reverberated through the door.

"Come in," I called, expecting either a patient or a delivery.

To my surprise, the door opened to reveal a young man in a sharp pilot's uniform that looked very professional. He stood tall and confident, his posture radiating an air of poise that was hard to ignore. Holding his cap under his arm, he exuded confidence that intrigued me and sparked my curiosity about his character. He was not just part of the crowd; he commanded presence and respect effortlessly.

His blend of confidence and composure caught my attention and made me want to explore his character and background further. I found myself increasingly drawn to his presence, as there seemed to be layers to him that warranted exploration. I became curious about the experiences that shaped him into who he is today. Ultimately, I felt an irresistible urge to engage with him and discover what lies beneath that intriguing exterior.

"Hello Doc," he said, his smile radiating warmth. *"Do you remember who I am?"*

I furrowed my brow, scanning his expression for any hint of understanding, yet nothing emerged. *"I'm truly sorry,"* I confessed, *"but I don't."*

He chuckled softly, a warm smile spreading across his face, his eyes glimmering with a mix of nostalgia and gratitude.

"That's alright, it truly is. It's been so many years since that fateful day. When I was just a little boy, you were my hero. You saved my life when I battled pneumonia so severe that I required ICU care. My parents were scared and unsure, but you offered not just treatment, but also hope. Your support was essential to my healing and personal growth, giving me the strength and confidence to recover and thrive. It has inspired me to broaden my horizons, dream bigger, and achieve many remarkable things. I can't emphasize enough how much your encouragement has meant to me as I navigated through challenges. Your belief in me has been a driving force in my success and fulfillment."

I was completely stunned, as the memory began to resurface slowly, like sunlight filtering gently through a partially drawn curtain. I remembered a frail boy who struggled to breathe. His anxious parents listened to my every word to find comfort in that difficult moment. I recall the long, sleepless nights of anxiously watching over him, hoping the difficult treatment would work. Before me stood this boy, tall and proud, a testament to the hope and effort surrounding him during tough times.

"I focused on my studies," he continued. *"I was determined to make the most of the second chance you offered me. Today, I am a pilot, and I just wanted to express my heartfelt gratitude... thank you."*

As he spoke, I felt a wave of emotions washed over me, a mix of pride, satisfaction, and deep gratitude. It was a moment that encapsulated the essence of my work. Evidence that the efforts I put forth can catalyze profound change in people's lives. I had saved many lives. Yet, witnessing the direct impact of my work in this way was a rare experience. It was deeply moving.

Seeing how my efforts helped someone achieve his dream was a powerful reminder. It showed how he overcame past challenges. This also highlighted the strength of healing and hope. It reaffirmed my belief in the impact of compassion and perseverance.

"Your journey is an inspiration, and hearing your story fills my heart with joy." I exclaimed.

I took a moment to appreciate our conversation's importance. I thought about the dedication and compassion I had poured into my work. My heart swelled with pride and joy, knowing that I had played a part in someone's journey towards his aspirations. As I reflected on this powerful reunion, I felt a renewed motivation to keep helping others. I wanted to help those who are still striving for their chance to succeed. It reminded me that even small efforts can make a difference in someone's life.

This unexpected visit reminded me of my purpose as a doctor. It reignited my commitment to heal both bodies and spirits. It also renewed my dedication to support individuals in taking back their lives. It is never just about treating sickness. It is about helping people enjoy life, follow their passions, pursue their dreams with courage, determination, even to fly!

Chapter 15
My first day as a Medical Intern

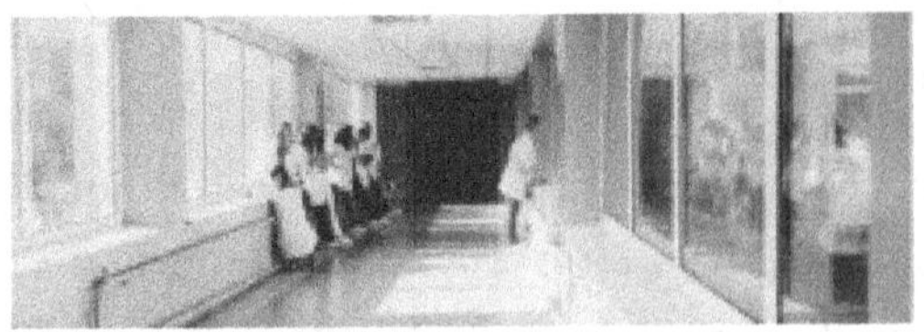

Prelude

On my first day as a medical intern, I experienced a whirlwind of emotions, from excitement to anxiety. Stepping into the hospital, I realized the importance of transforming theoretical knowledge into practical skills. Every patient encounter taught me invaluable lessons about resilience. I learned about the importance of connection and the privilege of caring for others. These lessons marked the start of my exciting journey in medicine.

First Day as a Medical Intern

I still vividly recall the whirlwind of emotions that engulfed me on my very first day as a medical intern. I wore my crisp white coat and stethoscope. I felt a mix of pride, excitement, and anxiety. These emotions made my heart race. Today celebrates years of hard work and dedication, bringing me closer to my dream of becoming a doctor. Yet, alongside that elation was a nagging feeling of navigating into the vast unknown, filled with both challenges and opportunities.

Now is the moment to transform my theoretical knowledge into practical skills. The moment has arrived to venture beyond the classroom and actively immerse myself as an apprentice in my chosen profession. This hands-on experience will not only deepen my understanding but also allow me to gain invaluable insights from seasoned professionals. Embracing this opportunity will pave the way for personal and professional growth in my career.

The hospital was busy. Patients sought care. Nurses attended to their tasks. Doctors moved purposefully through the crowded hallways. During my first internal medicine rotation, the senior resident welcomed me into the team, creating a valuable learning opportunity. I only had a notepad and strong determination. I felt excited to meet my first patients. Each one had unique challenges and stories. This marked the start of my medical journey, filled with great responsibility and exciting opportunities for personal and professional growth.

My first patient was a middle-aged man with uncontrolled diabetes, which brought me both excitement and anxiety. I nervously reviewed his chart, took notes, and prepared questions for the morning rounds with the team. As I presented my findings, my voice trembled, but I stayed focused on clearly explaining his symptoms and lab results. My attending physician listened carefully and gave helpful feedback, which improved my understanding and boosted my confidence for future presentations.

The day was an exhilarating blur of hands-on learning and practical experience. I drew blood for the first time. I listened carefully to heart and lung sounds. I managed several tasks under my seniors' supervision. I realized that textbook study couldn't prepare me for the emotional challenges of caring for real patients. Each patient has their own unique story. This realization deepened my appreciation for the art of medicine and the profound connections we forge with those we serve.

In the chaotic hospital ward, one moment truly resonated with me.

An elderly patient, grateful and hopeful, gently held my hand after I explained her treatment plan. *"Thank you, doctor,"* she said with a bright smile that lit up the room.

At that moment, I realized it was the first time anyone had called me *"doctor."* That simple expression of gratitude resonated with me, strengthening my commitment to medicine.

By the end of the day, I felt drained but strangely fulfilled from all the experiences I had. The hospital corridors, once intimidating, became a comforting second home for me. My first day as a medical intern had its challenges and mistakes. I realized it was just the start of an incredible journey. This journey would greatly impact my personal and professional growth. Each moment, each interaction, laid the foundation for a future I couldn't wait to explore.

This unforgettable day taught me important lessons. I learned about resilience, humility, and the privilege of caring for others. These lessons go beyond traditional medicine. It was a pivotal moment in my life, marking the start of a meaningful and compassionate journey. That day changed my understanding of serving and connecting with those in need.

This experience made me realize the importance of making a meaningful impact on others' lives. I've come to realize how much kindness and support can impact both individuals and the community as a whole. It reinforced my belief that small acts of generosity can lead to significant changes. Ultimately, it's essential to strive to make a positive difference wherever I can.

My journey into medicine began with a single step, marking a crucial moment for me. Entering this world of knowledge and compassion marked the beginning of an exciting journey. This decision marked the beginning of a lifelong quest to understand and help others through the healing arts.

I realized that this could open up many amazing opportunities in my medical career that I have only dreamed of. I am excited about the knowledge and skills I will gain to enhance my career. This could lead to significant personal and professional growth, and open doors to advancements in my field I never imagined. I am excited and eager for the many opportunities ahead as I start this journey.

Chapter 16
Unforgettable Moment in the Cockpit:

Prelude

The author recounts a memorable first cockpit experience during Army service in Kuala Lumpur. He remembered the excitement of sitting in the cockpit of a plane. This pivotal moment deepened appreciation for the universe's beauty, and reinforced gratitude and purpose in life, emphasizing every moment's significance.

Cockpit Experience

Some moments of our lives will stay in our memories forever, bringing joy and excitement long after they are gone. My first time in an airplane cockpit was unforgettable. I felt a mix of excitement and awe as I sat in the cockpit. I looked out at the vast sky. Being near the controls thrilled me. Experiencing the world from a unique perspective is a memory I will cherish forever. It was an unforgettable milestone that ignited my passion for aviation and adventure.

My journey truly began during my time while serving in the Army, which was a pivotal period of my life. I was on duty in Kuala Lumpur. I had the opportunity to board a C-120 plane for a flight from Kuala Lumpur to Labuan. To my amazement, this flight turned out to be an incredible experience, filled with unexpected moments. Everything felt familiar—the comforting hum of the engines and fellow soldiers settling into their seats reminded me of past flights.

I settled into my seat. I stored my bag under the seat. I buckled my seat-belt. I took a deep breath to calm my nerves for the exciting take-off. Just as I was getting ready for the flight, the captain of the plane spotted me.

He unexpectedly called out with urgency, *"Doc, please come to the cockpit!"*

This unexpected invitation made my journey more interesting. I wondered what the captain wanted from me. My excitement culminated in a blend of anticipation and curiosity about what awaited me in the cockpit.

Upon entering the cockpit of the plane, I was surprised by the complex instruments and controls around me. The dazzling array of screens and buttons, all meticulously arranged, created an exhilarating sense of adventure and possibility. I was excited to watch a complex machine in a world where technology and skill came together. The sight filled me with awe, reinforcing my wish to embark on this incredible journey through the skies.

The cockpit was a hive of instruments. It featured a myriad of dials, switches, levers, and buttons. These emitted a constant symphony of beeping noises, creating a complex orchestra of sound and light. From my seat behind the pilot, the view was stunning and unlike anything I had ever seen. The large windows revealed layers of clouds surrounding us, resembling endless oceans to the horizon. The pilot moved skillfully in the sky. This created an exhilarating sense of openness. I was left speechless and fully immersed in the beauty above.

I was captivated as the captain skillfully demonstrated the plane's controls, adjusting each instrument with precision. I was amazed as the plane effortlessly rose into the blue sky, defying gravity. A deep calm filled the cockpit despite the rumbling engines below, reminding us of the powerful machinery we were controlling. At that moment, I felt part of something beautiful and powerful. I soared above the earth in a unique dance of man and machine.

The experience of gazing down from above at my surroundings was truly unforgettable and left a lasting impression on me. I was captivated by the beautiful view of fluffy clouds drifting below me. Each cloud seemed to tell a story. It added to the beauty of the scene. The clouds enhanced the sense of wonder I felt at that moment. It was a magical sight that etched itself into my memory forever.

I admired the stunning scenery around me and particularly noticed a remarkable full circle rainbow in the sky. This rare phenomenon was stunning. Rainbows typically don't appear as full circles. The horizon blocks off half the view. The vibrant colors blended beautifully, creating a captivating show for anyone who looked up. It was a moment that felt almost magical, a stunning reminder of nature's beauty and wonder.

After we arrived in Labuan, I promptly took a moment to express my gratitude to the captain. I thanked him for his gracious hospitality and the warm welcome he extended to me. He didn't realize how meaningful that simple invitation to the cockpit was for me. It provided an experience that exceeded my expectations. My time in the cockpit enhanced my appreciation for planes and pilots, creating lasting memories I cherish. It was a unique experience that I will always hold dear in my heart.

It was an unforgettable journey into space that I will always cherish! This amazing experience made me realize the wonders of the universe and increased my appreciation for the beautiful planet. Every moment of the voyage was stunningly beautiful. Each part held deep significance. From the mesmerizing starry skies to the breathtaking views of Earth, the spectacle was awe-inspiring.

I returned home feeling grateful and full of wonder about the world and the endless possibilities beyond the atmosphere. It reminded me that there is a God. My existence here is both significant and precious. Every moment I spend here serves a purpose. As the Bible says, God is both creator and sustainer of the universe.

Life is a precious gift that deserves to be treasured. Acknowledging God brings a deeper meaning to my experiences and interactions. It inspires me to live with gratitude. It motivates me to live with purpose. It helps me appreciate every moment of my existence. It helps me recognize the value of my life. This perspective prompts me to stay aware and recognize the beauty in everyday experiences. By embracing this mindset, I aim to cultivate a life that is meaningful and purposeful. In doing so, I find joy and fulfillment in the journey I am on.

Chapter 17
Delivering Health Care in a Mobile Clinic

Prelude

In 1979, the author operated a mobile clinic in remote Taiping villages, providing essential healthcare to undeserved communities. The experience enhanced skills and fostered deep connections with grateful villagers. Despite challenging conditions, the work was rewarding. Heartfelt gestures, like shared food gifts, emphasized the profound impact of compassion and selflessness.

Mobile Clinic

In 1979, I was a young Medical Officer in the beautiful town of Taiping. It was surrounded by hills and greenery, giving it a peaceful feel. My official responsibilities seemed simple. Yet, they turned out to be much more rewarding than I expected. It became one of the most fulfilling experiences of my career. I ran a mobile clinic in remote villages near Taiping. I delivered crucial medical care to communities with limited access to healthcare. This role strengthened my professional skills. It deepened my connection to people's stories. This experience boosted my sense of purpose and commitment to my work.

The clinic was not adorned with luxury or extravagance, but it certainly fulfilled its essential purpose effectively. The government-funded van contained essential medical supplies and equipment to serve the community's health needs. My small, dedicated team worked well together to give care. It includes a skilled staff nurse, a helpful attendant cum dispenser, and a capable driver. We provided essential support to the villagers, who struggled to access medical services and had few healthcare options.

We started our journey at dawn each morning. We traveled along dusty roads and winding hills. Sometimes, we faced muddy paths from recent rains. We often visited remote villages hidden in dense jungles or far from main routes to help those in need. As the van entered the village, the atmosphere shifted noticeably. Our arrival felt as if it kicked off a lively festival of anticipation and hope. The excitement was palpable, as locals gathered to see us, their faces lighting up with joy and curiosity.

Men, women, and children gathered in large numbers, some traveling for miles to seek essential treatment. Many brought their elderly parents or held their young children, their eyes shining with hope for relief from their suffering. We handled various medical issues like fevers, wounds, infections, and chronic illnesses, often using only basic resources. My dedicated staff nurse handled wound care. She also provided immunizations. The attendant cum dispenser managed the medical supplies and medicines effectively. She also organized the busy crowd. We worked long hours without modern facilities.

I was deeply moved by the villagers' heartfelt gratitude, which shone through despite their limited means. Most of them didn't have any money to spare. Yet, their warmth and kindness were obvious. This was shown in the thoughtful gifts they left behind for us. After each visit, I found delightful surprises in our van. These included fruits like bananas, fresh vegetables, and even fish. There were also crabs, prawns, and frogs!

I joked with my driver, *"At this rate, we won't need to buy groceries; these villagers are so generous!"*

He chuckled but replied earnestly, *"They give what little they have, Doc. It carried profound meaning for them."*

And he was indeed correct in his assessment. The gifts symbolized deep trust, appreciation, and gratitude from people who, despite having little, generously shared what they could. These thoughtful actions showed their character. They built strong connections. These actions highlighted the powerful impact of generosity in our lives. In a world focused on material wealth, selfless giving reflects the true spirit of humanity.

Each day was exhausting, often leaving us sweaty and muddy. Yet, despite the challenges, we felt a strong sense of satisfaction on the drive back to Taiping. The smiles of the villagers we helped reminded us of the positive impact we were making. This rewarding feeling made all the long hours spent working and the bumpy roads we traveled seem trivial in comparison. It was a profound experience that reinforced our commitment to this important cause.

My time with the mobile clinic was incredibly fulfilling and transformative. The unassuming van represented far more than just a mobile clinic. It was a crucial link to those in need, showing how true compassion can overcome distance and obstacles. I often think about the modest gifts of fruits, fish, and frogs we received in gratitude. These heartfelt treasures will stay with me forever, reminding me of the impact we had on each other's lives.

Chapter 18
Tradition of the Army Regimental Dinner

Prelude

The author recalled his army service, emphasizing the strong friendships formed through shared traditions and the Annual Regimental Gala Dinner. This prestigious event showcased dedication and unity, celebrated achievements, and honored fallen comrades. The formal setting encouraged decorum, making each detail significant, while heartfelt speeches deepened connections and commitment within the military community.

A Trip Down Memory Lane

My memory took me back to my time of service in the army. I remembered when discipline, duty, and traditions helped build a strong sense of friendship in our community. A cherished tradition reminds me of the special moments. During these times, we built strong relationships through our dedication. Shared rituals brought us closer. The Army Annual Regimental Gala Dinner was a cherished tradition that symbolized unity and friendship during those memorable evenings. This annual gathering celebrated our achievements and strengthened our bonds, creating lasting memories that I cherished.

Officers attended this prestigious military event, wearing their best attire to leave a lasting impression. Each officer wore a perfectly pressed custom army uniform. It was decorated with medals and badges. These decorations showcased their dedication, years of service, and sacrifices made during their careers. Their uniform details highlighted individual accomplishments and reflected the pride of their military community.

The dining hall was a stunning sight as we entered, with every detail catching our eye. The tables were perfectly arranged, with silverware carefully placed, creating an elegant atmosphere. As we sat down, we realized that every detail mattered. This included our posture and the cutlery we chose for each course. Every detail in this setting was carefully planned, reflecting the effort put into making the dining experience memorable.

The atmosphere created excitement among the guests, suggesting a lavish dinner was on the way. Waiters moved gracefully around the room. They served exquisite soups, elegant roasts, and other delicacies. These dishes were presented as if they were works of art. In this lavish setting, conversations were rare. Even a small mistake in etiquette could lead to disapproving looks. Guests might get reminders to follow the traditions. The strict decorum and silent service created a surreal dining experience, shifting the focus from the food to social expectations.

During dinner, a deep silence fell over the gathering, interrupted only by heartfelt toasts and meaningful speeches that touched everyone. We stood up to honor our respected regiment and our country. We also remembered the fallen comrades who bravely served before us. Their sacrifices stayed forever in our memories. The powerful speeches reminded us of our responsibilities and the legacy we must uphold. Every word spoken brought us together, strengthening our commitment and the bonds we share in service and remembrance.

Everyone was truly delighted to enjoy the night together in each other's company. That year's Regimental Gala Dinner was more than just a formal event. It was a heartfelt celebration of our traditions. It also celebrated our camaraderie and shared values. It was a time to celebrate our shared history and strengthen our unity in all our efforts.

In that spirit, the gathering became a memorable testament to our collective commitment and mutual respect.

When I think about these events, I realize they are truly unforgettable experiences that have stuck with me over time. These dinners reminded me of our soldiers' discipline and unity, highlighting the times we stood together as one regiment. The formality and dignity of those gatherings evoke a deep feeling in me that is hard to express. Such cherished memories serve as a testament to the bonds we forged during these significant times.

Chapter 19

A Journey to Remember: Unexpected Luxury

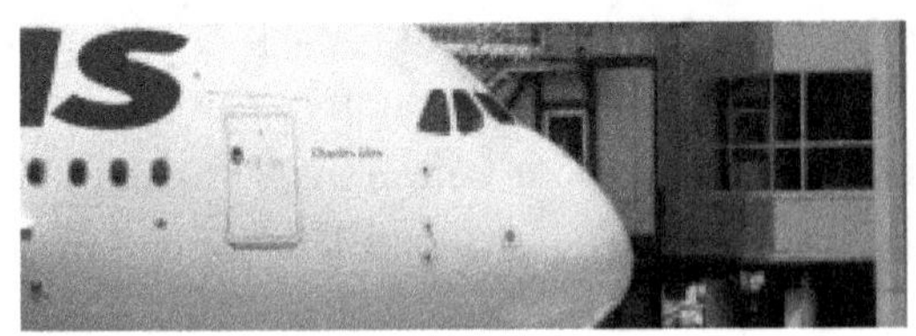

Prelude

The business trip started as routine. It transformed into a memorable experience. I discovered I was the sole passenger in the business class cabin. The exceptional service, luxurious meals, and tranquil atmosphere created a surreal journey. This unique experience reshaped my perspective on travel, leaving me with cherished memories to share for years.

A Journey to Remember

What began as a routine business trip turned into a memorable experience that I will cherish for a long time. As I sat in my plane seat, I noticed the unusual silence in business class. There was no chatter or the sound of champagne glasses clinking. Everything became clear. The air hostess approached me with a big smile. She hinted that something special was about to happen on this journey. This unexpected warmth and atmosphere hinted that this trip would be about so much more than just business.

"Welcome aboard!" she exclaimed with a warm and inviting smile, clearly excited about the journey ahead. *"It looks like we have the whole business class cabin to ourselves. We can enjoy plenty of space to relax and have a great flight."*

I can't wait to settle in and experience everything this cabin provides!

"What? Am I the only passenger in this entire cabin?" I exclaimed in disbelief. *"I can't believe it; I'm the only one here!"* My surprise was real as I tried to understand how I could be alone in this cabin.

She said with a smile, *"Yes, you have everything you need!"*

As I stepped into what I imagined was a perfect paradise, a thrill of excitement coursed through me. The sight of rows and rows of inviting, plush, luxurious seats spread out before me was simply mesmerizing. I comfortably sank into my seat and casually dropped my bag because it felt so inviting.

"Keep me posted if anything comes up!" she said with a playful glint in her eyes, handing me the bottle of sparkling wine.

Her sly grin suggested a shared secret, making the moment feel even more special. I wondered what she was thinking as I took the bottle, feeling the anticipation in the air between us.

The benefits of traveling in business class became even more obvious to me with each delicious course that arrived. The menu was extensive and included many luxurious dishes that usually make me hesitate. I indulged in rich lobster bisque and succulent wagyu beef. I also enjoyed a variety of decadent desserts. It all felt like a lavish feast truly fit for royalty. Each bite reminded me of the exceptional experience that comes with this level of comfort and service.

After the meal, I found myself exploring the fleeting world of leisure and entertainment. I watched a collection of movies. I rested my feet comfortably on my lap and enjoyed the moment of peace. I tested various lie-flat positions to evaluate their comfort and relaxation suitability. This combination of cinematic escapism and comfort-seeking made my breaks truly rejuvenating.

The service I received was exceptional and truly outstanding in every way. The air hostess treated me with such attentiveness. I felt like a VIP. It was as if my needs were the only ones that mattered. Snacks appeared out of nowhere. My drink was generously refilled. This made my time even more enjoyable.

The plane soared through the sky. I paused to appreciate the stunning view of the fluffy clouds outside my window. Flying felt magical, with the soothing engine hum and soft, warm cabin lights creating a calming atmosphere. Each moment felt wondrous and peaceful, making me feel both small and deeply connected to the vast sky above.

The airplane door opened. I stepped onto the tarmac.

The air hostess joked, *"Hope you enjoy your private cabin."*

"Oh, yes," I laughed. *"This could ruin the economy for good!"*

My experience was so strange and surreal. It felt like I had entered a different reality. It was a major shift that changed how I see things. I will share this amazing story, with all its details, for many years to come.

Chapter 20
Exploring Theology: Bible College of New Zealand

Prelude

The author reflected on his transformative experience at the Bible College of New Zealand from 1999 to 2002. During this time, a postgraduate diploma in Theology deepened his understanding of spirituality. He engaged with diverse peers and faced challenging academics. This fostered lasting friendships and personal growth. These experiences ultimately shaped his belief and life perspectives significantly.

Bible College of New Zealand

I attended the Bible College of New Zealand in Auckland from 1999 to 2002. I pursued a postgraduate diploma in Theology. Strong faith and a wish to learn drove this important decision. These motivations led me to explore the realm of theology and spirituality. I didn't realize how much this experience would change my perspectives, values, and understanding of myself and the world.

The campus was lively, especially among the Asian community, who thrived in the energetic atmosphere. Every corner buzzed with lively conversations in a mix of languages, discussing theology, culture, and the complexities of life. The diverse students from around the world added a unique richness to the experience, offering a variety of perspectives. It started as just a study space. It evolved into a lively mix of global beliefs. It also reflected shared human experiences.

Mornings began with prayer meetings in the peaceful chapel. People came together to unite their diverse traditions and backgrounds for a common purpose. These gatherings not only set a reflective tone for the day but cultivated a sense of community among us. The lectures built on a spiritual foundation. They were intellectually challenging and explored biblical exegesis, church history, mission, pastoral care, spiritual formation, and systematic theology in depth. The professors and lecturers were experienced scholars and passionate educators who encouraged critical thinking and expanded our understanding.

Assignments were central to my studies, each offering a unique challenge to explore scripture and its profound truths. In this endeavor, the library quickly transformed into my second home, a sanctuary of knowledge and inspiration. I was surrounded by tall bookshelves filled with valuable ancient commentaries, thoughtful theological journals, and essential reference materials. Days blurred together as I spent hours studying, crafting essay ideas, and preparing for exams.

Despite the demanding academic environment, the surrounding community was lively and welcoming. The Asian students took the initiative to organize potluck dinners, showcasing delightful flavors and dishes from their homelands. We enjoyed spicy curries, savory dumplings, and fragrant rice dishes. We sat around the table. We shared heartfelt stories about our countries and cultures. We also talked about how God had uniquely guided each of us on this journey. This experience created strong bonds that overcame language barriers and built lasting friendships, enriching our lives long after college.

Occasionally, there were moments of struggle that felt almost insurmountable. Late nights grappling with tough theological ideas left me exhausted. The stress of looming deadlines made me feel homesick. Yet, through all these challenges, there emerged a profound sense of purpose that fueled my journey. The knowledge I gained during this time was not merely academic. The experience was transformative and life changing. Every lecture, workshop, tutorial, discussion, and assignment deepened my understanding of God's word. They revealed its practical applications in my life and ministry goals.

Graduation day in 2002 proved to be a truly bittersweet moment, encapsulating years of hard work and dedication. Wearing my cap and robe and proudly holding my diploma, I looked out at the familiar faces. My professors, lecturers, tutors, classmates, family, and friends who had supported me throughout my journey. The students came from different places, each with their own unique stories. Now, as they face new beginnings, they were ready to live out their faith in meaningful ways.

This day was a poignant reminder of the achievements behind me and the exciting challenges that lay ahead. Those three formative years at Bible College were not just about the attainment of a diploma. They were an important journey that prepared me for a greater purpose in the future. During this time, I faced many enriching and challenging situations that significantly shaped my character, beliefs, and spiritual growth. This unique journey had valuable experiences and friendships. It is an unforgettable part of my life. It continues to inspire me daily.

The lessons and strong relationships I built during my early years have greatly shaped my personal and professional life. These experiences have shaped my perspectives and decisions, leaving an indelible mark on my path ahead. I often think about the relationships and knowledge I gained, appreciating their lasting impact on who I am today. The significance of those moments continues to resonate with me as I navigate the future.

Poetic Grace
Footprints of Time

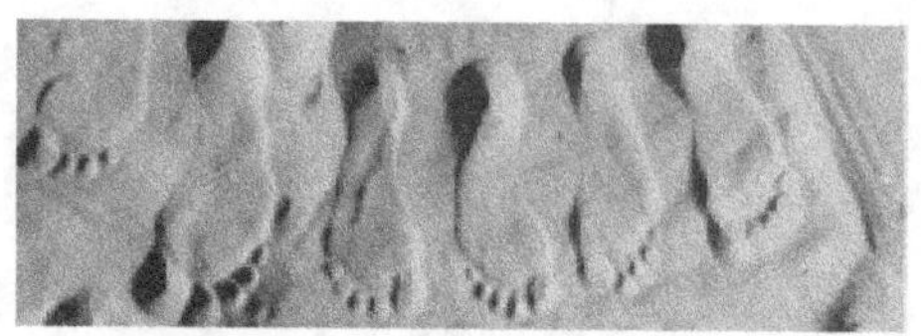

I walk on footprints
Beneath the endless skies
Every step is a sign
For yours and mine
I have memories that passed me by
From mountains deep to valleys high
I walk below the deep blue sky
A dust trail, a whispered call
I leave traces, for one and all
The memories of life, slip and fade
On the sand, my footprints are laid
As if shadows were cast on stone
I find myself, yet not alone
In every place, a narrative sleeps
Laughter, sorrow, and love that weep
Momentary dreams and hopes that climb
Every footstep that will rhyme
Walk with me through days I haven't told
The sunlit walkways and nights so cold
Let me leave my footprints on the sand
As I walk the street hand in hand
Time will pass, as all things do

The trace of my presence will carry through
The map of my heart forever bound
My Footprints will still be found

Poetic Grace
A Journey of Nostalgia

Through the fading mist of yesteryears
I wander through the fading years
When memories bloom like flowers bright
Where time is a soft and gentle light
The road I walk is overgrown
I still whisper what was known
There is laughter and quiet sighs
Above the summer and winter skies
A song from childhood, a passing breeze
Golden light shining through the trees
The taste of rain, the smell of pine
Dance in echoes, for yours and mine
Faces blurred but still remain
Soft as the threads of a picture frame.
Every smile a spark, every tear a seed
From which I feed and planted deep.
I close my eyes and there I stand
The child returns with dreams unplanned
With infinite hopes and endless skies
Before the world started to rise
The clock will tick, the years will fly
But in my heart those moments lie

The treasure chest of joy and pain
They are calling me home again
The road will twist and wind
The past always lingers behind
The journey of the heart embrace
With every step I find my place
When the night seems too long.
I will sing that old song
The journey of nostalgia and grace
Leads me back to where I stay

Poetic Grace
Down Memory Lane

Down memory lane
Where shadows dance and moments reign
The echoes of ancient time
Singing the familiar soft rhyme
The street is long, the sky is grey
But in my heart, it is as bright as day
Every step I walk, I will see again
The now, the then, the why, and the when
The park where children's laughter swirled
The place where dreams unfurled
The smell of rain on a sunlit skin
Enjoy the living deep within
I stop to listen and hear the sound
The soft voice of love unbound.
A friend's smile, a lover's glance
The magic of an elusive chance
Old oak trees standing tall
Branches reaching out from all
I carved my name and soul
On every knot, a story whole
The years passed and turned their page
I feel the pulse of the same age

A strong heartbeat, a fire bright
What never dims is what burns bright
Down memory lane where time stands still
I carry everything with love and will
In my heart they will stay
Ghosts from yesterday's sweet day
As I walk, I am filled with grace
Down memory lane is where I stay
The past and the present are intertwined
When all is lost, and all is divine

About the Author

Dr. Andrew C. S. Koh is a Christian author with an impressive portfolio of 55 published books. He is a writer, blogger, podcaster, Bible teacher, digital creator, and medical director. He studied theology at Laidlaw College in Auckland, New Zealand, and now lives in Malaysia with his family. He set a record in the Malaysia Book of Records for publishing the most books In 2021.

Bringing Faith to Life Through Inspiring Stories and Timeless Truths

Author of From Stethoscope to Wisdom:

https://storyoriginapp.com/giveaways/a517155c-75a2-11ef-a813-bbd0e34c8b27

Link Tree:

https://linktr.ee/andrewcskoh

Universal book link:

https://books2read.com/ap/xX066D/Dr-Andrew-C-S-Koh

New Release Notification:

https://books2read.com/author/dr-andrew-c-s-koh/subscribe/1/384961/

Free Books:

https://storyoriginapp.com/giveaways/b295be58-7736-11ec-ac4b-e34d930c508e

Also By

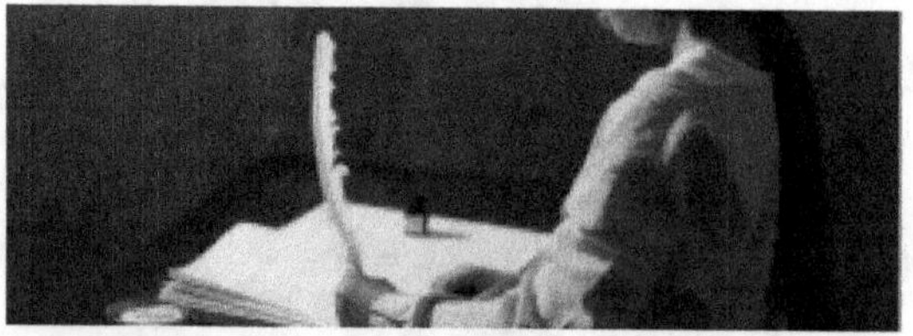

The Hourglass Paradox: Destiny is Never Linear

Root: Daily Devotions for Deepening your Faith

Whispers of Grace: Poems of Heartfelt Reflection

Journey in Rhyme: Poems of Reflection

Mapping the Heart: A Doctor's Reflection

From Stethoscope to Wisdom: A Doctor's Reflection

Footprints in Time: A Journey of Nostalgia

The Forgotten Melody: A Story of Redemption and Hope

Time Traveller's Return: Back to 1969

From Slavery to Freedom: Moses and Exodus

From Creation to Covenant: A Journey through Genesis 1-11

From Man to Mission: Abraham and Birth of a Nation

From Pit to Palace: Faith, Dreams, and Destiny

From Deceiver to Destiny: Jacob's Story

From Slave to Brother: Discovering redemption in Philemon

From Symbols to Salvation: An Epic Odyssey in Revelation

One Last Thing

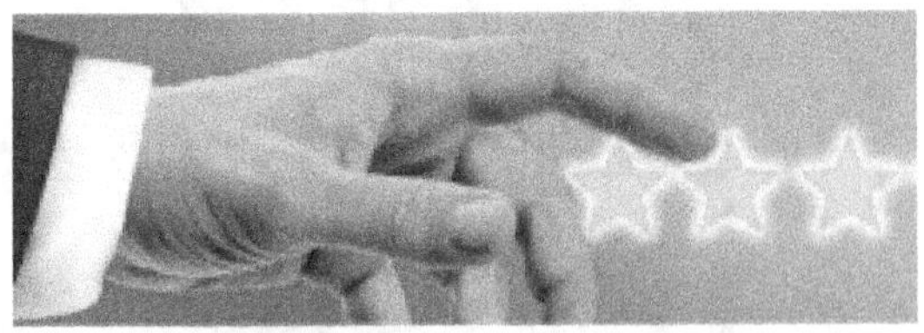

Thank you for selecting my book. I genuinely hope it has offered you an enjoyable and stimulating experience. I would appreciate your feedback and would be grateful if you could write a review on the platform where you bought it or on a book review site. Your feedback will help others make choices and show me which parts of the book were effective or lacking. Your honest review will help me grow as a writer and motivate me to create more engaging stories in the future.

Thank you once again for taking the time to explore my book. I genuinely hope it proved to be a rewarding experience for you. Your support means everything to me, and I am truly grateful to each reader who joins me on this journey. Together, we can cultivate a vibrant community of readers and writers united by our love for storytelling.

Each review contributes to a vibrant dialogue that enriches our literary experience. I look forward to hearing your thoughts and insights as we continue to explore the depths of creativity together. Your feedback is invaluable, and it inspires me to keep pushing the boundaries of my writing. Let's keep the conversation going and delve deeper into the stories that connect us all.

Scan the QR code above to get a review copy of Footprints in Time

Scan the QR code above to discover.

Don't miss out!

Visit the website below and you can sign up to receive emails whenever Dr Andrew C S Koh publishes a new book. There's no charge and no obligation.

https://books2read.com/r/B-A-FMXV-JWTLF

BOOKS2READ

Connecting independent readers to independent writers.

Did you love *Footprints in Time*? Then you should read *From Stethoscope to Wisdom*[1] by Dr Andrew C S Koh!

[2]

From Healing Hands to Divine Wisdom.

From Stethoscope to Wisdom explores the intersection of medicine, faith, and personal growth. Dr. Andrew C. S. Koh, blending his experience as a doctor with profound spiritual insights, offers a transformative journey toward deeper wisdom and purpose. A compelling read for those seeking holistic healing in mind, body, and spirit.

From Stethoscope to Wisdom delves into the powerful convergence of medicine, faith, and personal development. The author skillfully combines medical knowledge with deep spiritual insights, leading readers on a transformative journey to greater wisdom and

---

1. https://books2read.com/u/3nPEVK

2. https://books2read.com/u/3nPEVK

purpose. This book is a captivating read for anyone seeking holistic healing for their mind, body, and spirit—a true must-read!

Read more at https://www.drandrewcskoh.com.

Also by Dr Andrew C S Koh

Bible Study
From Creation to Covenant
From Deceiver to Destiny: Jacob's Story
From Slavery to Freedom
From Man to Mission
From Slave to Brother
From Symbols to Salvation
From Legalism to Liberty
From Tribulation to Triumph

Daily Devotion
Manna of Life: Daily Devotion

Daily Devotions
Bread of Life Daily Devotions
Words of Eternal Life
Bread From Heaven: Daily Devotions
Light of the World Daily Devotions
Light of the World Daily Devotions
The Way, the Truth, and the Life

Rooted: A Daily Devotion to Deepen your Faith

Fiction
The Hourglass Paradox

Genesis
Understanding Genesis 1-11: From Adam to Abraham
Faith Journey of Abraham: Genesis 12-25
Life Story of Jacob: Genesis 26-36
The Story of Joseph: Genesis 37-50
From Pit to Palace

Gospels and Act
The Gospel According to Matthew
Daily Devotion Gospel of Mark
The Gospel According to Luke
Daily Devotion Gospel of John
Acts: Volume 1 and 2, From Jerusalem to Rome
From Galilee to Golgotha

Non Pauline and General Epistles
Hebrews: the Just Shall Live by Faith
1 John, 2 John, 3 John & Jude: a Verse by Verse Bible Study
General Epistles: 1 Peter, 2 Peter, James

Pauline Epistles
Romans: The Just Shall Live by Faith
1 Corinthians
2 Corinthians
1 Thessalonians, 2 Thessalonians, Philemon
Pastoral Epistles: 1 Timothy, 2 Timothy, Titus
Galatians: Justified by Faith in Jesus Christ
Philemon: Charge to the Master's Account

Prison Epistles
The Prison Epistles
Philippians: Rejoice Always in the Lord
Colossians: He is the Image of the Invisible God
Ephesians: Every Spiritual Blessings

Reflective Poems
Journey in Ryhme: Poems of Reflection
Whispers of Grace

Standalone
Apocalypse: Understanding the Book of Revelation
Expository Preaching
Memoirs of a Doctor
Moses: Let My People Go
Living Word Living Savior
From Stethoscope to Wisdom

Walking in His Footsteps: A Pilgrim's Journey
Mapping the Heart
The Forgotten Melody
Footprints in Time
From Love to Light
Time Traveller's Return
The hourglass Paradox

Watch for more at https://www.drandrewcskoh.com.

About the Author

Dr Andrew C S Koh a retired cardiologist, Bible teacher, and author of 50 titles. With a passion for making Scripture come alive, he blends theological insight with practical life application to help readers grow in faith and understanding. His writing reflects a deep commitment to God's Word, forged through decades of medical service, spiritual study, and personal devotion. Dr. Koh's works have encouraged believers around the world to walk closer with Christ and live out their calling with purpose and conviction.

Koh's unique perspective blends his extensive knowledge of the medical field with his deep theological insights. He studied theology at Laidlaw College in Auckland, New Zealand. He now calls Malaysia home, where he lives with his family. He made history in 2021 by setting a record in the Malaysia Book of Records for publishing the most books in a single year.

Whether he's teaching the Bible, creating digital content, or sharing his thoughts through various media, Dr. Koh's mission is clear: to make the Word of God accessible and relevant to everyday life. His works aim to inspire believers to grow deeper in their faith, live with purpose, and embrace the transformative power of God's love.

Link tree:

https://linktr.ee/andrewcskoh

https://books.drandrewcskoh.com/link-tree

free ebook:

https://storyoriginapp.com/giveaways/b295be58-7736-11ec-ac4b-e34d930c508e

Read more at https://www.drandrewcskoh.com.